MAN WITH A BROKEN HEART.

written and illustrated by Jim Brancaleone

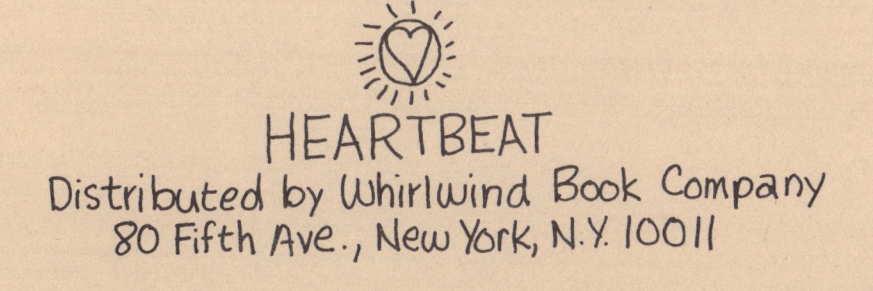

HEARTBEAT

Distributed by Whirlwind Book Company
80 Fifth Ave., New York, N.Y. 10011

Copyright © 1976 by Jim Brancaleone

All rights reserved under International and Pan-American Copyright Conventions.

Please do not reproduce any portion of this book without the written permission from the publisher.

Library of Congress Catalog Card No. 77-72049

ISBN 0-9601186-1-6

First Printing: May, 1976
Second Printing: March 1977

Printed in the United States of America

Back cover photo: Robert McCabe, N.Y.C.
Cover typography: Typographics Plus, Inc., N.Y.C.
Printing: Ellner Printing Co. Inc., N.Y.C.

Distributed by Whirlwind Book Company
80 Fifth Ave., New York, N.Y. 10011

Published by HEARTBEAT
34 King Street, New York, N.Y. 10014

To the woman
who broke my heart.
And opened it.

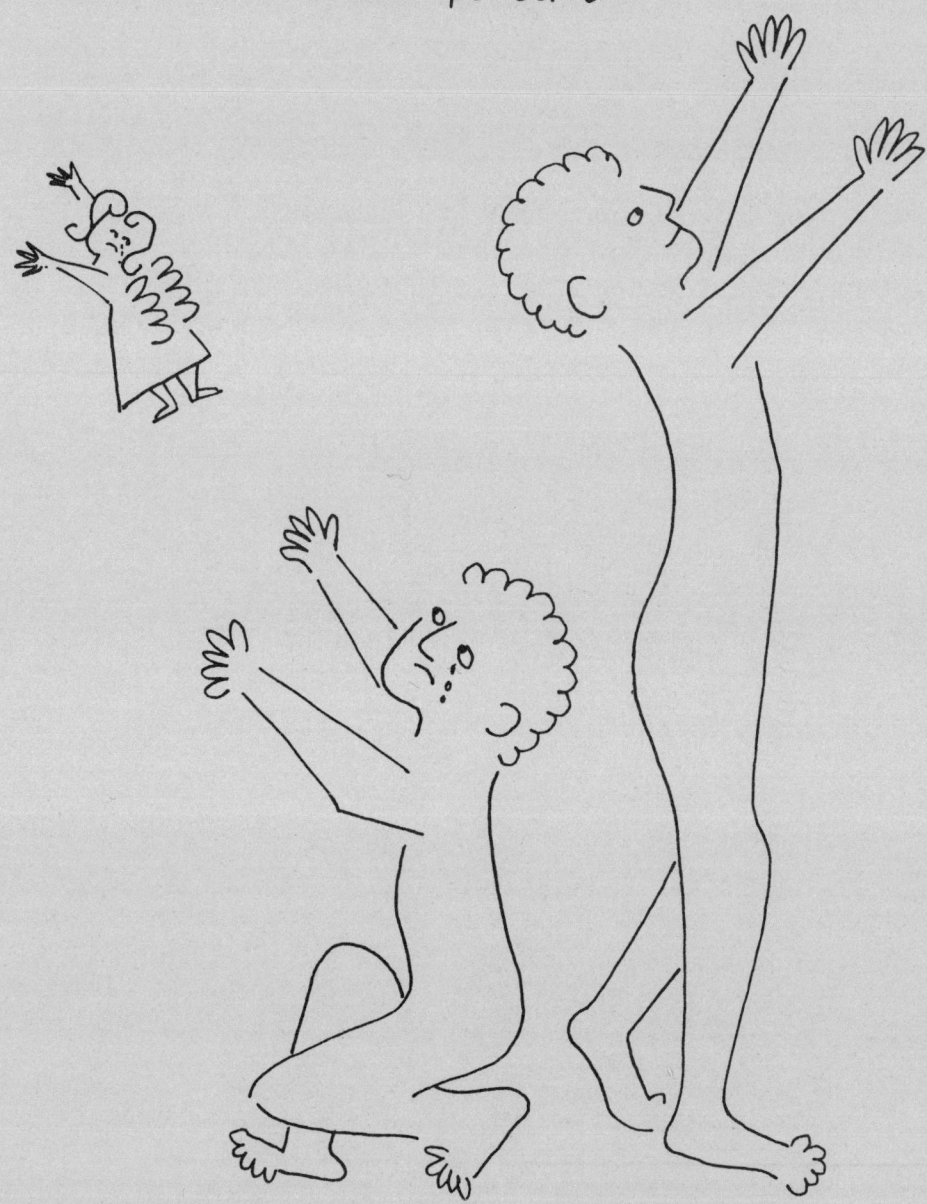

Chapters
1. FALLING IN LOVE
2. THE HEART BREAK
3. LONELINESS
4. RECOVERY

1
Falling in Love

Before I met her all I knew about love was how to live without it.

Fate must have brought us together.

But it wasn't easy getting to know each other.

Then one day something happened.
There were no boundaries, no horizons.
We were flowing.

Truthfully, the sex was a bit unnerving.

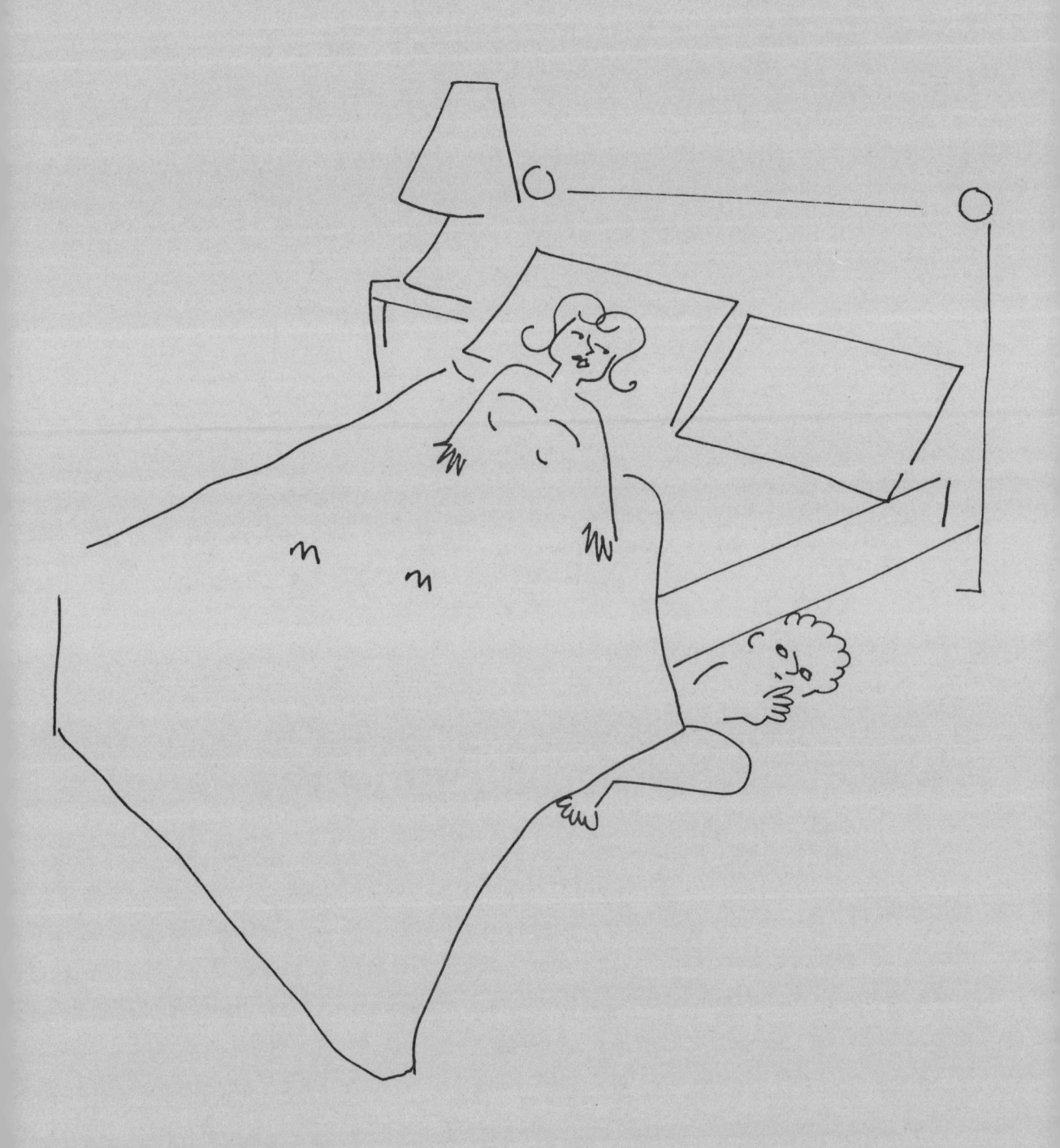

That soon changed.
We'd share time, space, everything.

It was such a relief not to be lonely.

Her cooking was delicious.

Her loving superb.

Sharing my dreams, fears and frustrations was so comforting.

A world I once felt left out of,
I now felt part of.

The dull ordinary days were now full of surprises.

The long nights full of intimacy.

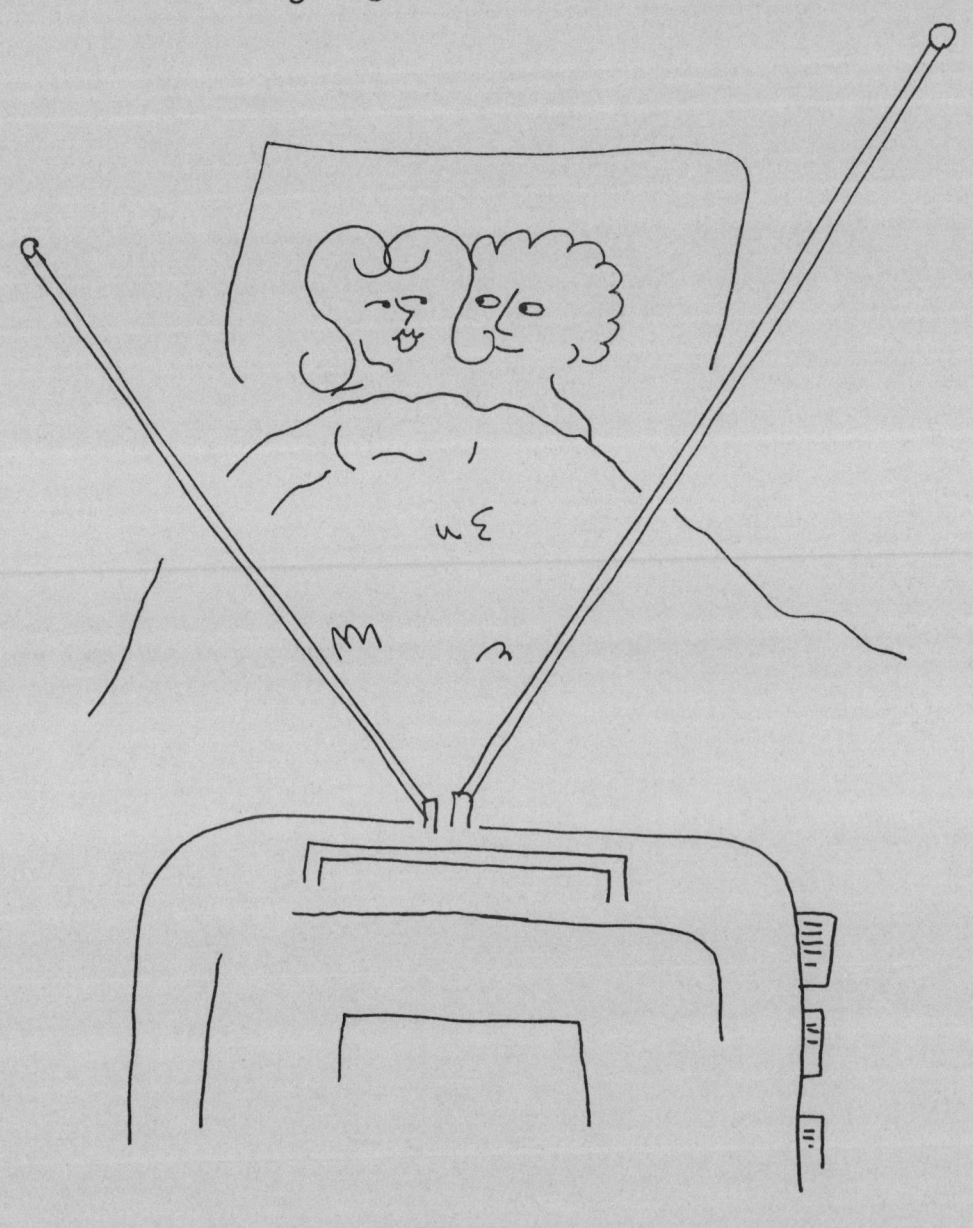

We were going to live happily ever after.

I didn't plan on a change of weather.

2
The Heart Break

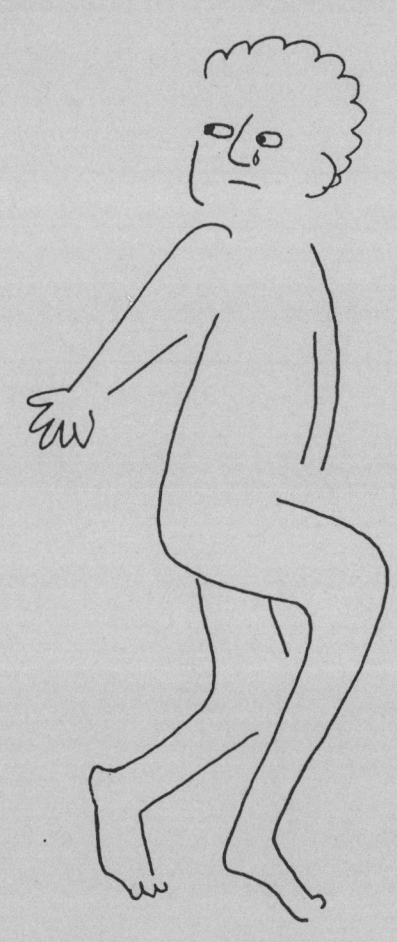

One night I went to bed with a headache and woke up with a heartache.

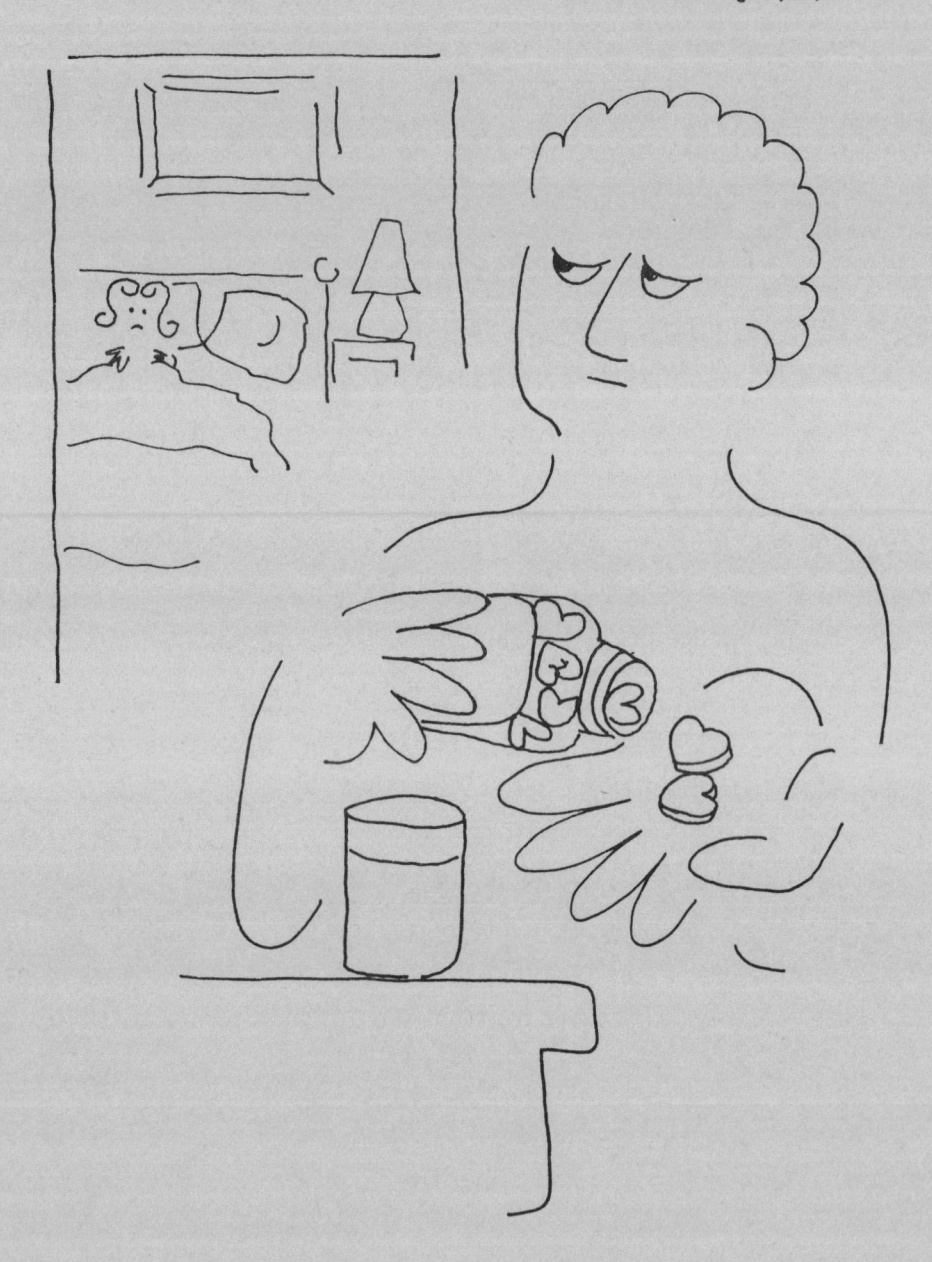

Something had changed.
As we grew, we grew apart.

We couldn't agree on the simplest things.

There was no more affection.

Our home turned cold.

It was agony being so close,
yet feeling a million miles away.

Conversations ended in arguments.

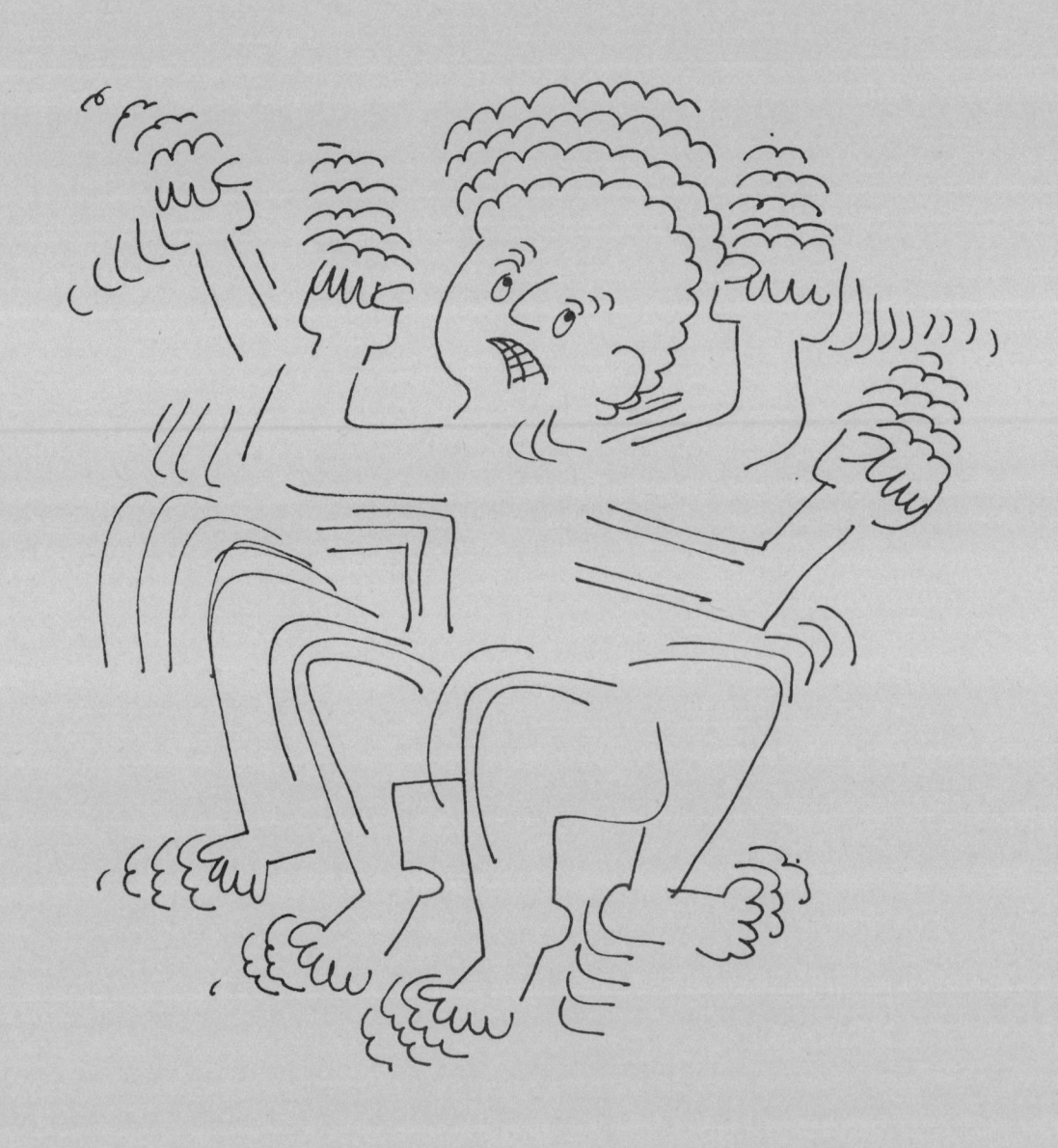

Or died in silence.

Bills to pay, dirty dishes, dirty laundry. Everything was trudgery.

All we had to share
was aggravation and despair.

Loneliness is such a sad affair.

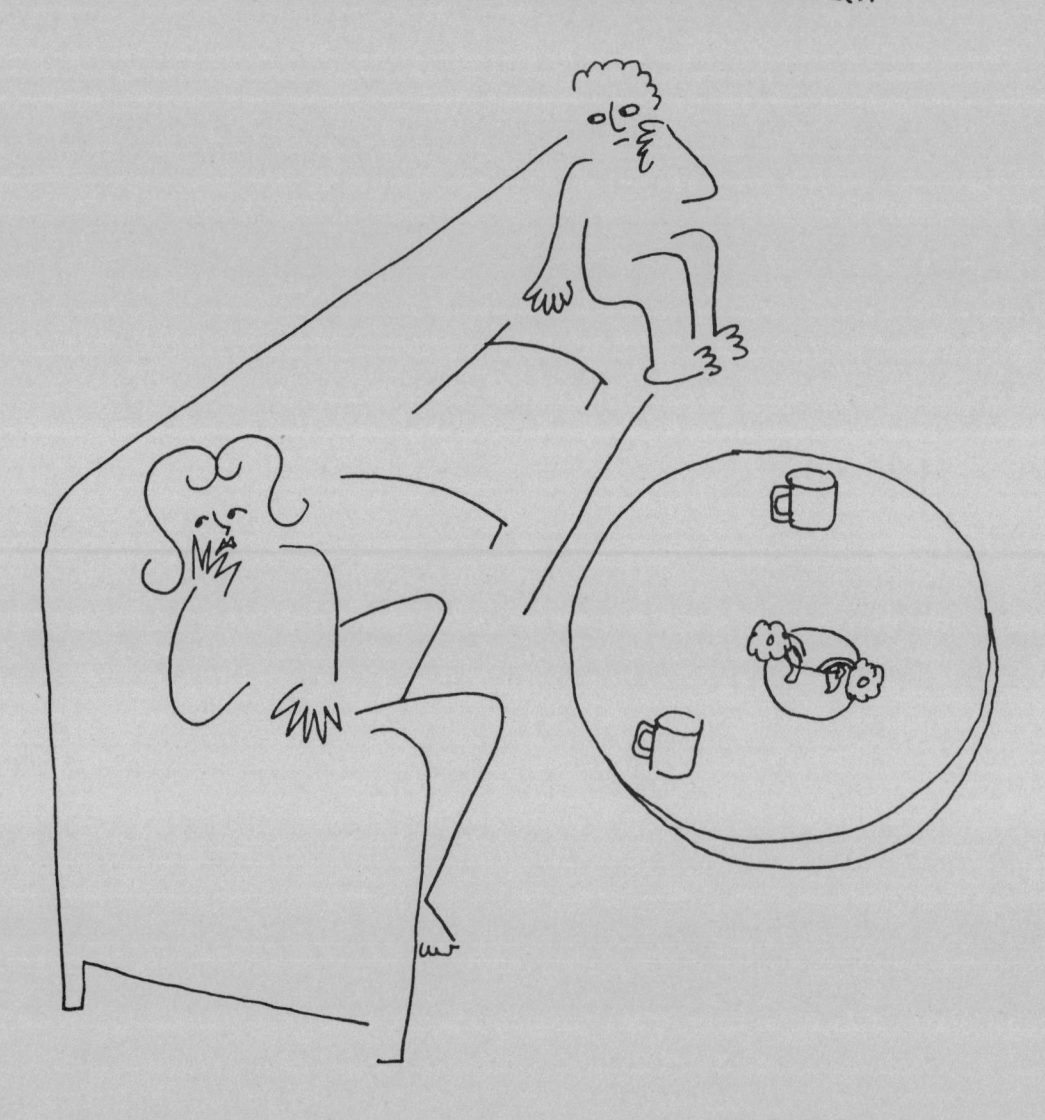

I couldn't love her or leave her.

She left. She was braver.

3
Loneliness

I always dreamt
of what it would be like falling in love.
I never imagined the end.

when she left she took all of me.

There was no one to share my life with.

Or satisfy my desires.

My world expired.

In vain I rehearsed for her return.

My love letters went unanswered.

I lost my strength.

I couldn't hide the hurt inside.

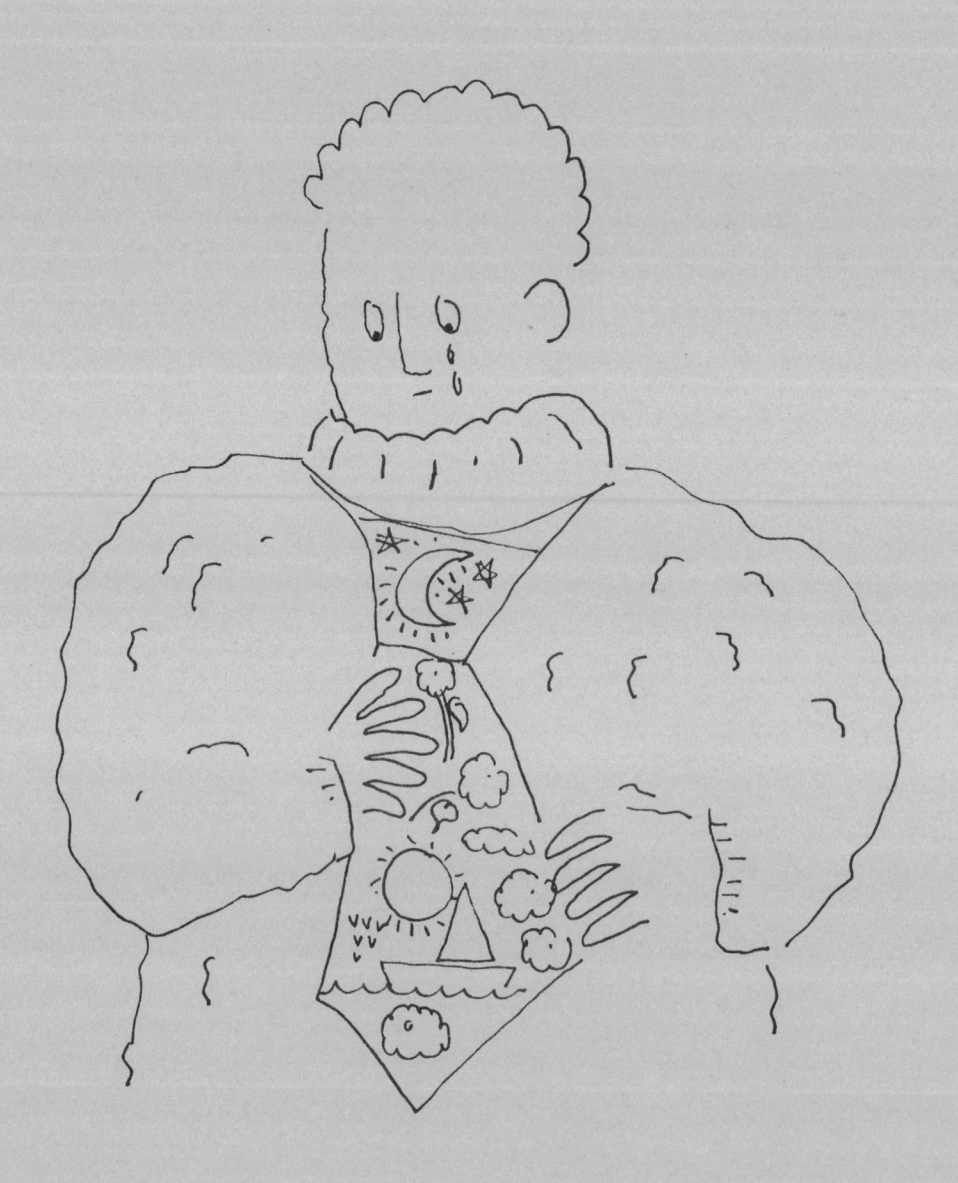

Where ever I traveled the heart break followed.

Everywhere I turned she was gone.

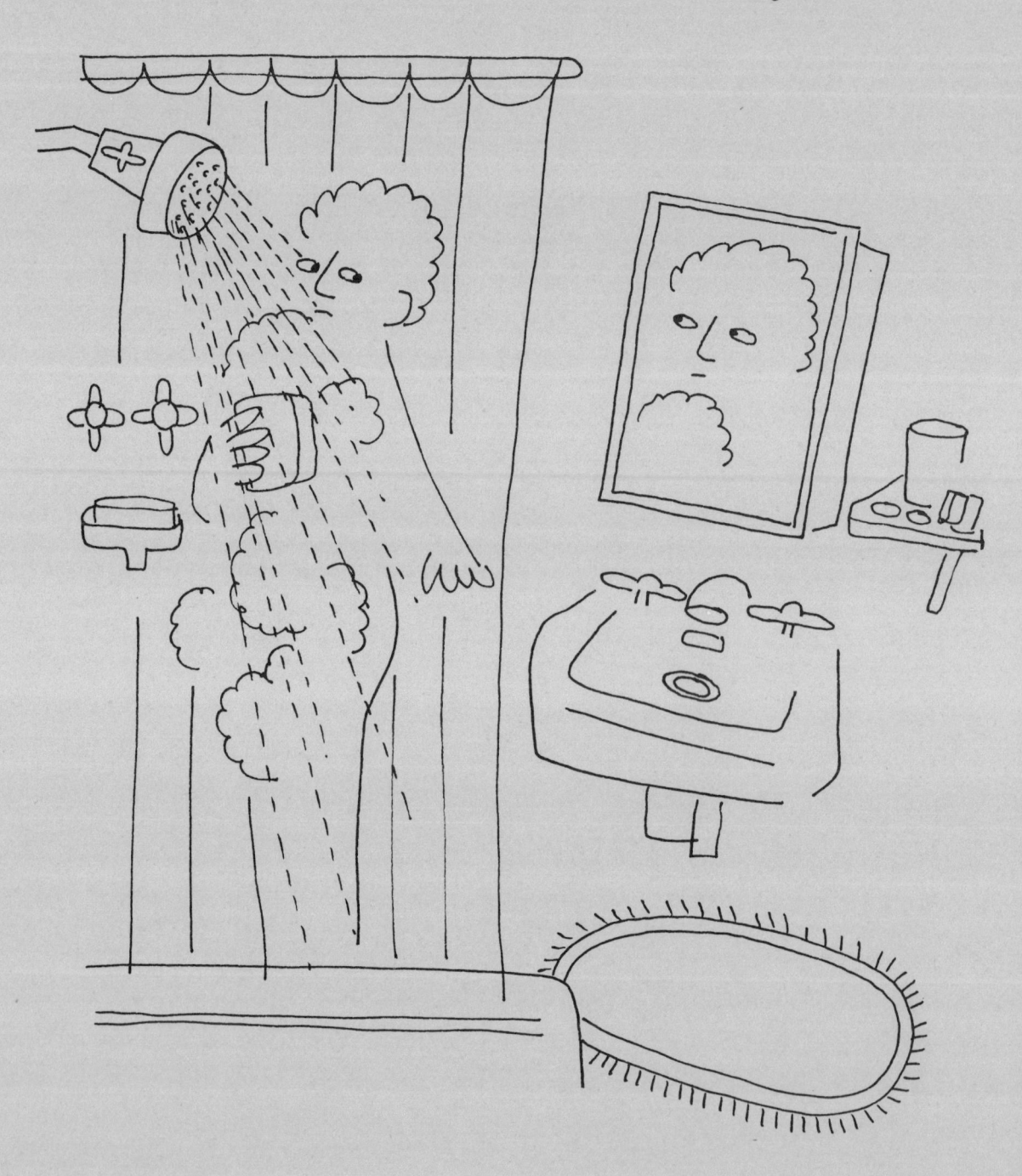

I played the game wrong.

Holidays, birthdays, free days
one day was worse than the other.

The loneliness was unbearable.

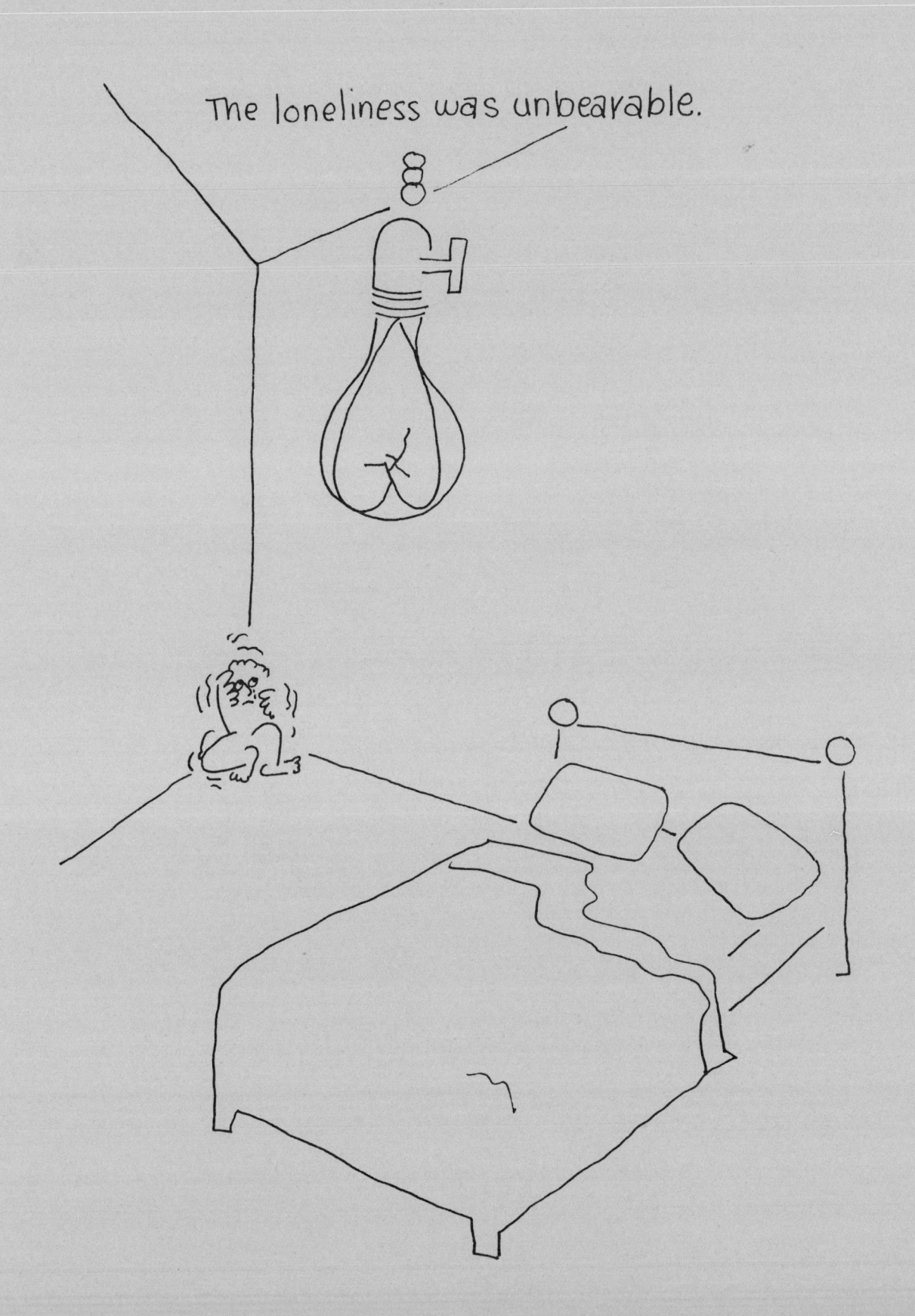

I was disposable.

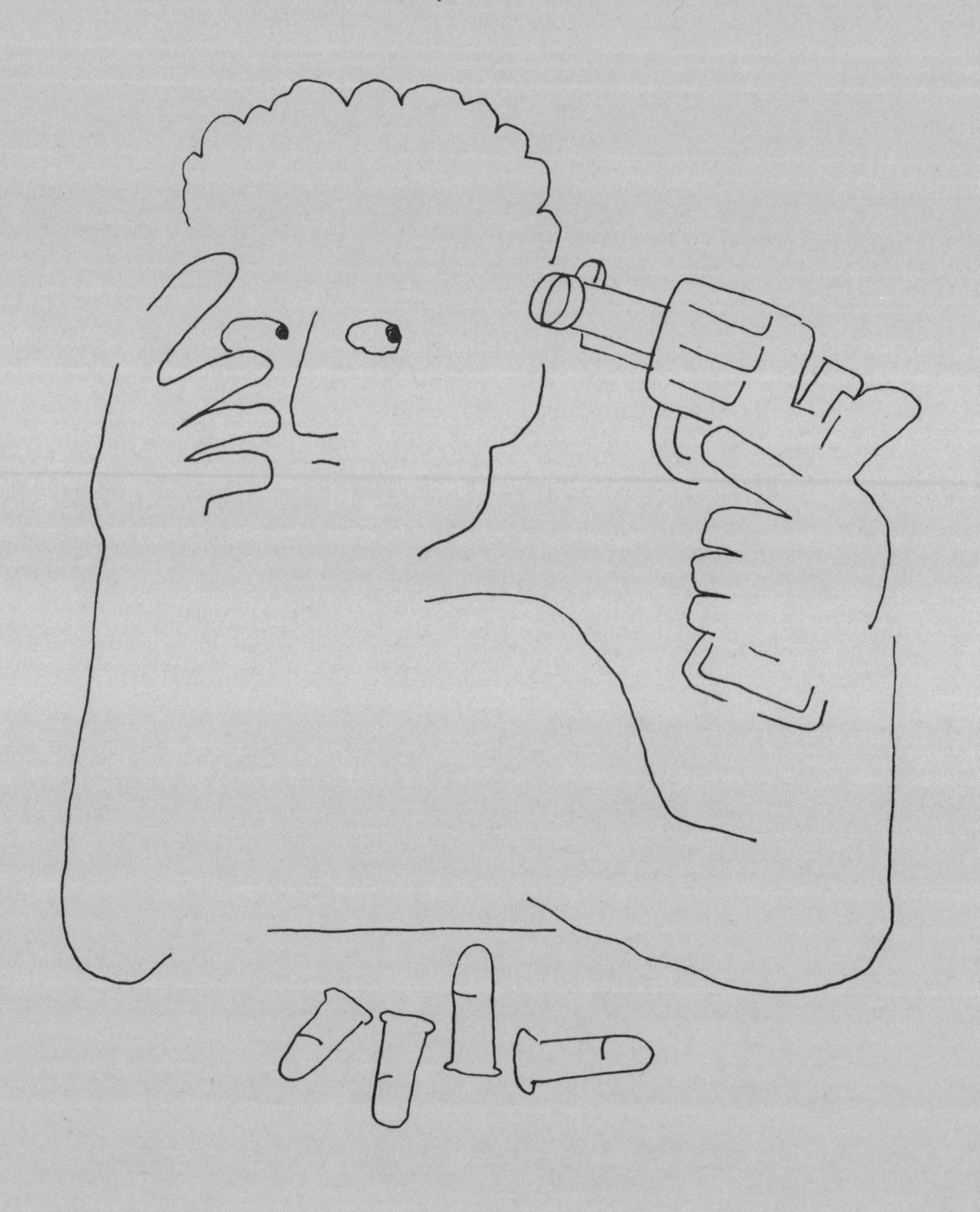

4
Recovery

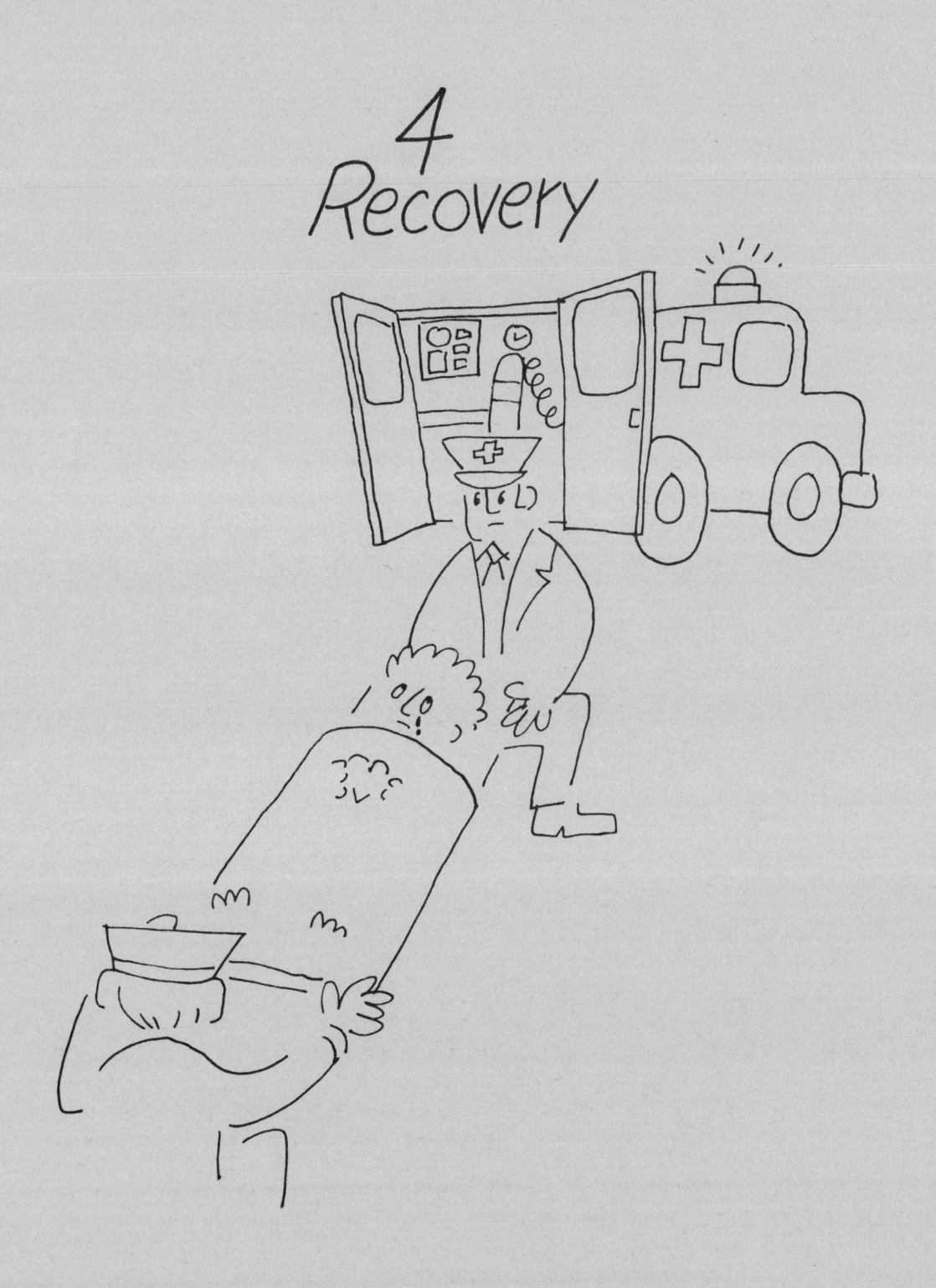

I felt doomed until a little tenderness
helped me out of the gloom.

Repairing the damage.

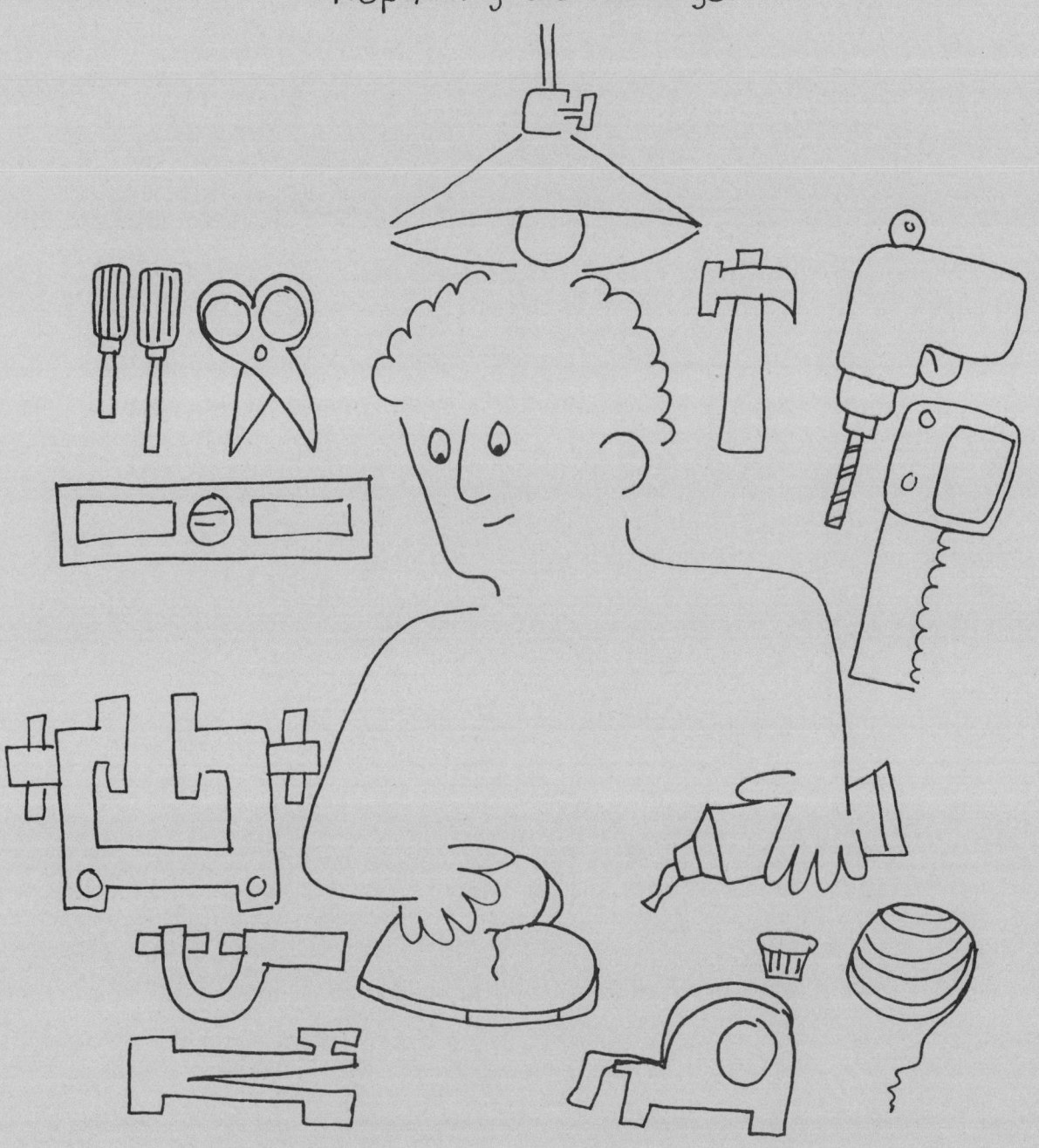

Looking at my faults and growing.

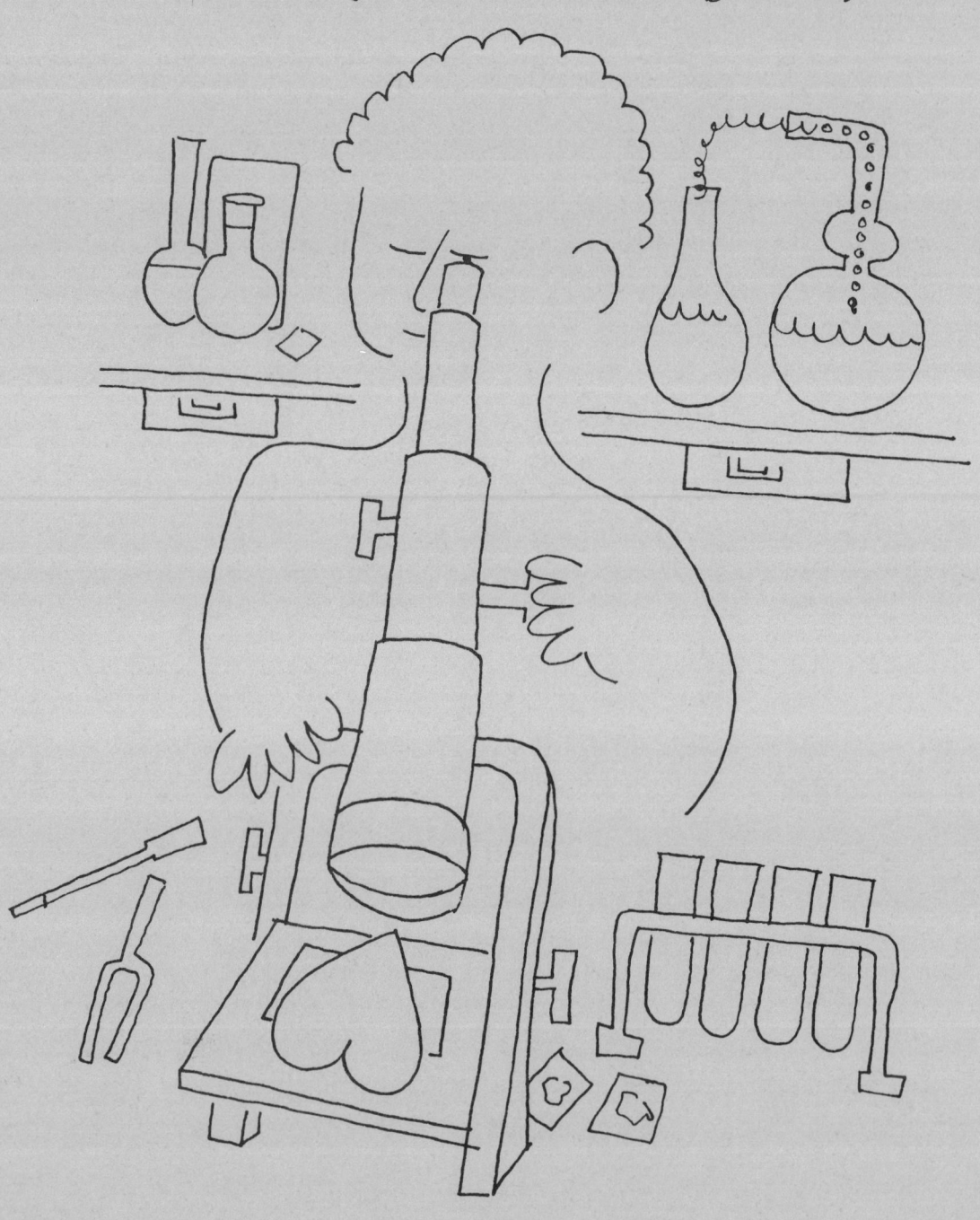

In time blossoming.

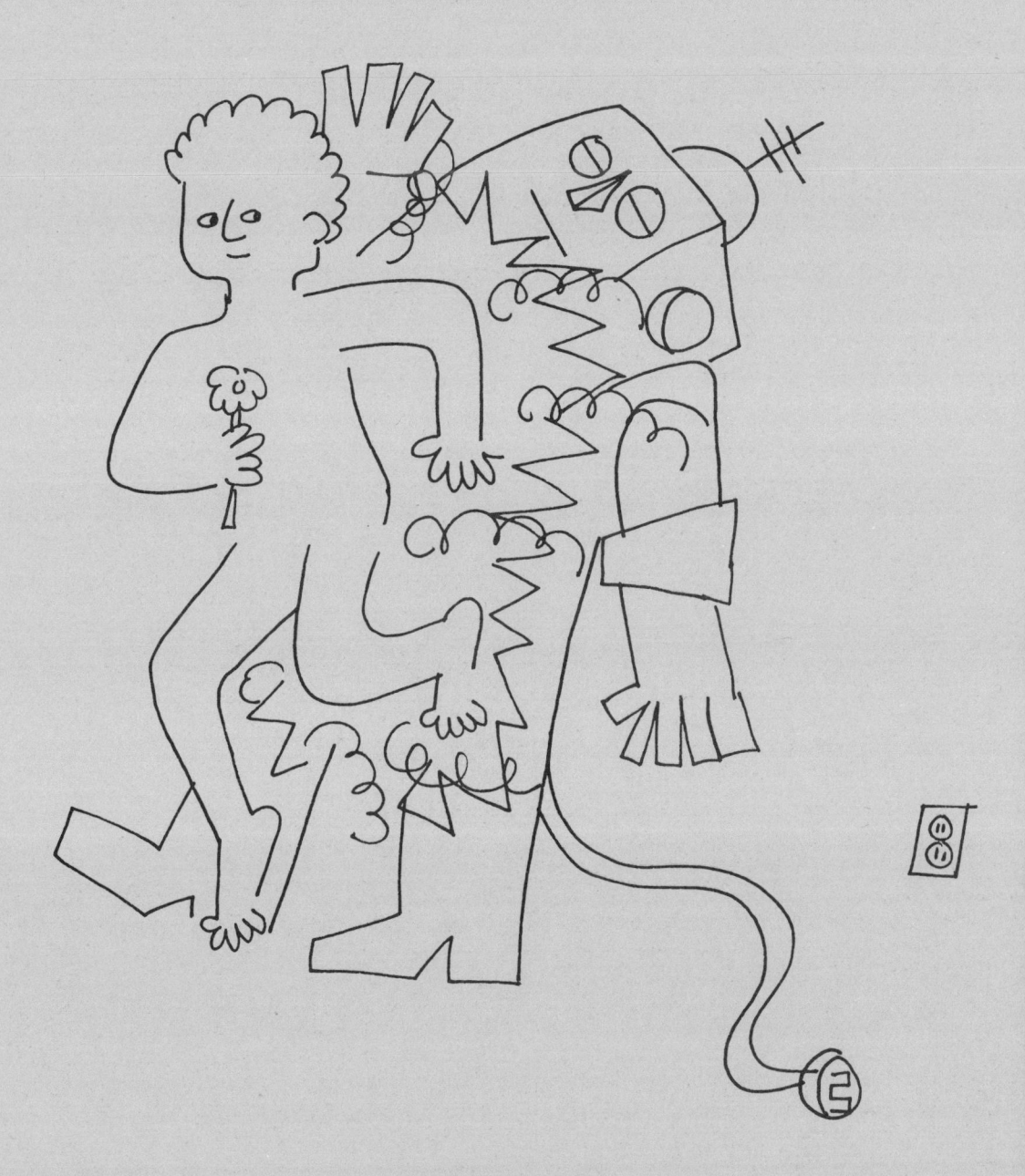

I found myself.

Feeling like I never felt before.

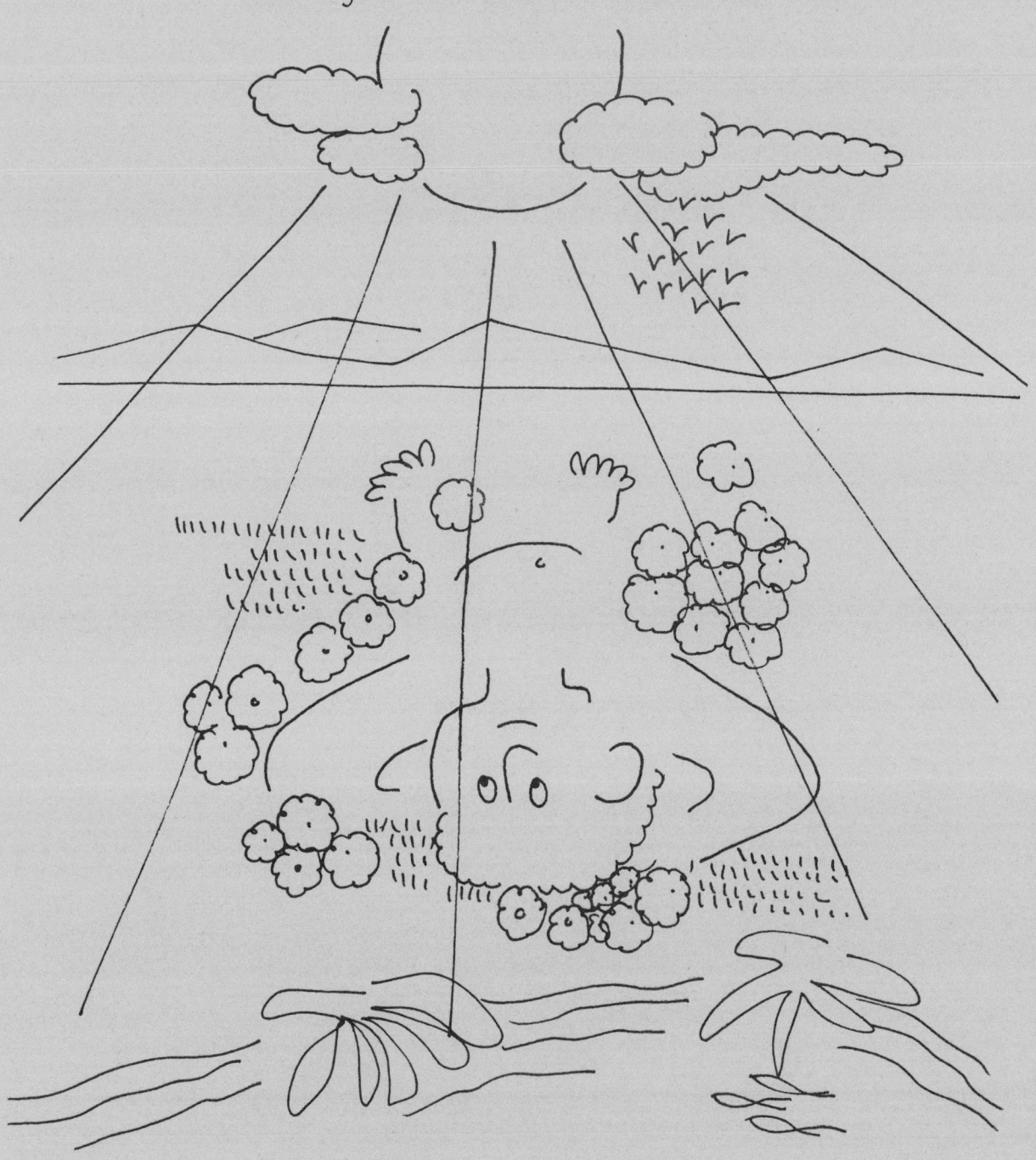

Spending the days in creative ways.

The evenings reading, watching TV and making her recipes.

Slowly getting over old memories.

Openly sharing my feelings with lovely human beings.

Falling in love again wasn't as easy.

The days got brighter.
I even discovered room in my heart to love
the woman who caused me to suffer.

The Beginning